Math and Critical Thinking Challenges

For the Middle and High School Student

By

Reza Nazari

Copyright © 2017

Reza Nazari

All rights reserved.
No part of this publication may be reproduced, stored in a retrieval system, or transmitted in any form or by any means, electronic, mechanical, photocopying, recording, scanning, or otherwise, except as permitted under Section 107 or 108 of the 1976 United States Copyright Ac, without permission of the author.
All inquiries should be addressed to:

www.effortlessmath.com
info@effortlessmath.com

ISBN-13: 978-1548465056

ISBN-10: 1548465054

Effortless Math Learning Center

13601 Preston Road #W788

Dallas, TX 75240

Contents

Introduction 6

Section One: Number Properties 9

Section Two: Ratio, Proportion and Percentages 27

Section Three: Algebra 34

Section Four: Geometry..57

Section Five: Intelligent Math 75

Section Six: Other Topics 90

Answers 96

Introduction

This book is for all teachers and parents who wish to make their students and children intelligent and smart. It is very possible for all students to excel in Math!

A super collection of more than 120 problems challenge your students in all areas of math—from basic arithmetic to algebra – while emphasizing problem-solving and critical thinking. It's the perfect refresher course on all math subjects we all encounter in our daily lives.

The problems and the critical thinking questions in this book are prepared to challenge even the best students in the nation. This is also a problem-solving textbook for students in grades 5 - 12 who are preparing for advanced Math contests like the Harvard-MIT Mathematics Tournament.

Written for the gifted math students, the new math coach, the teacher in search of problems and materials to challenge exceptional students, or anyone else interested in advanced mathematical problems.

I recommend it to any students who aspire to be "great problem solvers."

A strong foundation in pre-algebra is necessary before approaching most of the problems in this book. You or your student should not get discouraged if you cannot solve most of the problems. The challenging problems are supposed to be very difficult even for super smart students!

If your students could solve most of the problems in this book, they are definitely as smart as the world's smartest students.

Reza Nazari
January 2017

Section One: Number Properties

Challenge 1

What is the average (arithmetic mean) of all the multiples of ten from 110 to 990 inclusive?

- A. 480
- B. 500
- C. 550
- D. 590
- E. 600

1. Critical Thinking

How many squares are there in a chess board?

64? 65? No! Consider squares of 2 × 2, 3 × 3, etc.

Challenge 2

1- $(1+\frac{1}{2}) \times (1+\frac{1}{3}) \times (1+\frac{1}{4}) \times (1+\frac{1}{5}) \times \ldots \times (1+\frac{1}{2015}) =$

A. $\frac{2015}{2014}$

B. $\frac{2016}{1001}$

C. 1008

D. 2015

E. 2016

2. Critical Thinking

$1 = 5^1$
$2 = 5^2$
$3 = 5^3$
$4 = 5^4$
$5 = ?$

? ? ?

Challenge 3

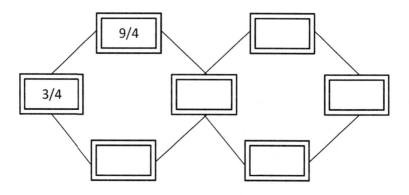

2- In the figure above, the sum of the values of the numbers inside two rectangular that connected with a line equals to three (For example 3/4 + 9/4 = 3), what is the sum of numbers inside all rectangular?

A. $9\frac{1}{4}$

B. $9\frac{3}{4}$

C. $11\frac{1}{4}$

D. $11\frac{3}{4}$

E. 12

Challenge 4

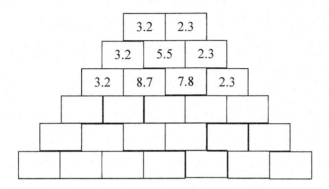

In the figure above, if the pattern continues, what is the sum of the values in all of the rectangles on the base? (Sum of 7 rectangles)

A. 121
B. 137
C. 157.7
D. 170.5
E. 176

Challenge 5

Number 4 is a perfect square number (2 × 2 = 4) and number 8 is a perfect cube number (2 × 2 × 2 = 8). How many positive perfect square numbers less than 2016 are also perfect cubes?

A. 2

B. 3

C. 4

D. 5

E. 10

Challenge 6

In a children's game, students count from 1 to 100 and applaud every time that they find either a multiple of 3 or a number ending with 3. How many times are they supposed to applaud?

- A. 30
- B. 33
- C. 36
- D. 39
- E. 40

3. Critical Thinking

When number y is divided by 7, the remainder equals to the quotient. What is the greatest value of y?

Challenge 7

If $a = (5^{11})^2$ and $b = 4^{11}$, how many digits long is ab?

A. 22

B. 23

C. 33

D. 44

E. 121

Challenge 8

The number 10 has four different factors: 1, 2, 5, 10. What is the smallest 2 digits number that has exactly three positive factors?

Challenge 9

How many positive integers less than 10,000 are there in which the sum of the digits equals 5?

(A) 31
(B) 51
(C) 56
(D) 62
(E) 93

Challenge 10

If $a=2^{6000}$, $b=3^{4000}$ and $c=7^{2000}$, which of the following is true?

A. $a<b<c$
B. $c<b<a$
C. $a<c<b$
D. $c<a<b$
E. $b<a<c$

Challenge 11

How many positive integers less than 1000 do not have any 5 as any digits?

A. 700

B. 728

C. 736

D. 770

E. 819

4. Critical Thinking

12 = 13

35 = 28

47 = 311

10 = ?

Challenge 12

How many digits are used to write the number 20^{10}?

A. 10

B. 11

C. 12

D. 13

E. 14

Challenge 13

If t and $\sqrt{w}$ are inversely proportional when t = 2 and w=9, what is the value of t when w = 2?

Challenge 14

If $a^x = \dfrac{2}{3}$, what is the value of a^{-3x}?

A. $\dfrac{2}{27}$

B. $-\dfrac{2}{27}$

C. $\dfrac{8}{27}$

D. $-\dfrac{8}{27}$

E. $\dfrac{27}{8}$

5. Critical Thinking

In how many three digits numbers, the hundreds digit is equal to the sum of other digits? (Numbers such as 321 or 514)

Challenge 15

Which of the following is neither a perfect square number nor a perfect cube number? (A perfect square is a number that can be expressed as the product of two equal integers. For example, 4 is a perfect square number. 2×2=4

A perfect cube is the result of multiplying a number three times by itself. For example, 27 is a perfect cube number. 3×3×3=27)

    A. 2^9

    B. 3^8

    C. 4^7

    D. 5^6

    E. 6^5

Challenge 16

What digit appears in the units place in the number obtained when 2^{136} is multiplied out?

A. 0
B. 2
C. 4
D. 6
E. 8

Challenge 17

How many numbers between 400 and 600 begins with digit 5 or ends with digit 5?

A. 20
B. 100
C. 110
D. 120
E. 140

Challenge 18

$4^{20} + 4^{20} + 4^{20} + 4^{20} = ?$

A. 4^{120}

B. 16^{30}

C. 4^{30}

D. 2^{40}

E. 2^{42}

Challenge 19

If $t^{\frac{1}{2}} = p^{\frac{-2}{3}}$ and $p^{\frac{1}{5}} = z^{\frac{-3}{5}}$, what is the value of t in terms of z?

Challenge 20

If n is a perfect cube number and n = 2700m, what is one possible value of m?

Challenge 21

If $y = 7 \times 10^{83} + 3$, what is the remainder when y is divided by 9?

   A. 0

   B. 1

   C. 2

   D. 3

   E. 4

Challenge 22

If $\sqrt[6]{x} = 6$, then $\sqrt{x^6} = ?$

A. 6

B. 6^3

C. 6^9

D. 6^{18}

E. 6^{24}

6. Critical Thinking

If 20% of 35% of $\frac{2}{3}$ of variable x equals to 15% of 12% of $\frac{3}{2}$ y, what is the value of x in terms of y?

Challenge 23

$(2^{89} - 2^{88})(2^{77} - 2^{76}) =$

A. 2^2

B. 2^{76}

C. 2^{77}

D. 2^{88}

E. 2^{165}

Section Two: Ratio, Proportion and Percentages

Section Two

Ratio, Proportion and Percentages

Challenge 24

The current ratio of girls to boys at a certain school is 2 to 7. If 10 additional girls were added to the school, the new ratio of girls to boys would be 3 to 8. How many girls currently attend the school?

    A. 22

    B. 32

    C. 42

    D. 56

    E. 112

Challenge 25

20 liters of 40 percent antifreeze in fuel are mixed with 40 liters of 10 percent antifreeze in fuel. The percentage of antifreeze in the new solution is:

A. 15%

B. 20%

C. 25%

D. 30%

E. 35%

7. Critical Thinking

$$(1-\tfrac{1}{2}) \times (1-\tfrac{1}{3}) \times (1-\tfrac{1}{4}) \times ... \times (1-\tfrac{1}{100}) = ?$$

Challenge 26

The sale price of a computer with 20% discount is $20 cheaper than its price with 15% discount. What is the original price of the computer?

Challenge 27

The ratio of sugar to flour for cooking a cake is $\frac{1}{2}$ to 2. What percent of the cake is flour? (Assume that there are only sugar and flour in the cake)

    A. 50%
    B. 60%
    C. 70%
    D. 80%
    E. 90%

Challenge 28

During last three years, the price of a car is reduced by 10% in the first year, 20% in the second year, and 25% in the third year. What percent of the original price is the total reduction of the car's price?

    A. 36%

    B. 40%

    C. 46%

    D. 54%

    E. 55%

8. Critical Thinking

If $5^x + 5^{x+1} + 5^{x+2} = \dfrac{31}{25}$, what is the value of x?

Challenge 29

In a certain village, the ratio of adult men to adult women is 3 : 5 and the ratio of adult women and children is 2 : 7. What is the ratio of adults (men and women) and children?

A. 10 : 7
B. 7 : 10
C. 2 : 5
D. 16 : 35
E. 6 : 15

9. Critical Thinking

The average of five numbers is 11 and the average of eight numbers is 7.75. What is the average of these 13 numbers?

Challenge 30

The product of two numbers is 216 and their sum is 35. What is their difference?

10. Critical Thinking

Amanda and Dani can paint a room together in 6 hours. If Amanda can paint the room by herself in 8 hours, what percent of the painting does Dani do?

Section Three: Algebra

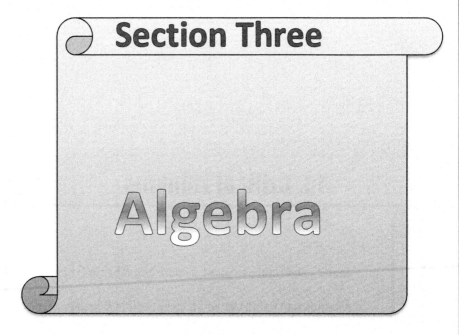

Challenge 31

Sophia has a guitar lesson three times a week and Lukas has a Math lesson every other week. In a given term, Sophia has 40 more lessons than Lukas. How many weeks long is their term?

- A. 8
- B. 12
- C. 16
- D. 20
- E. 24

Challenge 32

If 8 workers can build a house in 20 days, how many workers is needed to build the house in 4 days?

- A. 12
- B. 26
- C. 32
- D. 40
- E. 44

Challenge 33

12 years is the difference between Alex's age and Ron's age. If the ratio of their ages is 3:5, what is the sum of their ages?

   A. 20
   B. 30
   C. 48
   D. 60
   E. 66

Challenge 34

$464 is divided among Janet, Elliot, and Sarah. Janet received $\frac{2}{3}$ of Elliot's money and Sara received $\frac{2}{5}$ of Janet's money. How much money did Janet get?

   A. 64

   B. 100

   C. 160

   D. 240

   E. 280

11. Critical Thinking

What is the degree between hour and minute hands at 6:30 AM?

Isn't it 0? No!

Challenge 35

The ratio of the ages of Eric and Tara is 2 to 3 and the ratio of the ages of Tara and Marshall is 9 to 7. If the sum of their ages is 66, then how old is Eric?

Challenge 36

In a small farm, there are 8 hens, 5 chickens, and 4 roosters. A hen eats 2.5 times of a chick and a rooster eats 1.5 times a hen. If all together eat 4000 seeds per day, how many seeds does a hen eat during one day?

   A. 250
   B. 280
   C. 300
   D. 350
   E. 400

Challenge 37

Alice bought two books with $\frac{2}{5}$ of her money and bought 4 pencils with $\frac{2}{9}$ of her remaining money. If the price of each book was $15, what was the price of each pencil?

- A. $1.00
- B. $2.50
- C. $4.00
- D. $6.50
- E. $8.00

Challenge 38

200 percent of a half of $\frac{1}{5}$ of a tank is full of gas. If 90 gallon of gas is added to the tank, half of it will be filled. What is the capacity of the tank?

  A. 150 Gallon
  B. 180 Gallon
  C. 200 Gallon
  D. 260 Gallon
  E. 300 Gallon

Challenge 39

Joe and Mark can finish a job together in 100 minutes. If Joe can do the job by himself in 5 hours, how many minutes does it take Mark to finish the job?

   A. 120
   B. 150
   C. 180
   D. 200
   E. 220

Challenge 40

What is the average of three numbers if the sum of the first and second number is $\frac{11}{5}$, the sum of the second and third number is $\frac{31}{15}$, and the sum of the first and third umber is $\frac{7}{3}$?

A. $\frac{13}{15}$

B. $1\frac{1}{10}$

C. $\frac{18}{15}$

D. $2\frac{1}{5}$

E. $6\frac{3}{5}$

Challenge 41

The price of two pounds of apple is $2.55 less than the price of the same apple. What is the price of 4 pounds of apple with the same rate?

   A. $2.55
   B. $2.85
   C. $3.00
   D. $3.20
   E. $3.40

Challenge 42

Mr. Ronald is 53 years old. He has three children, John 14 years old, Nicole 9 years old and Mark 4 years old. In how many years, the age of Mr. Ronald will become equal to the sum of his children's age?

Challenge 43

David can finish a job in 54 days. Peter is 35% faster than David. How long does it take Peter to finish the same job?

- A. 38
- B. 40
- C. 44.2
- D. 50
- E. 52

12. Critical Thinking

What is the next number?

3, 7, 23, 87, ... ?

Challenge 44

Edward can finish 40% of a job in 2 days and Emanuel can finish 15% of the same job in 3 days. How many days does it take Edward and Emanuel to finish 75% of the same job if they work together?

    A. 2.5

    B. 3

    C. 4.5

    D. 5

    E. 5.5

Challenge 45

The average of 14 numbers is 18 and the average of 18 numbers is 14. What is the average of all 32 numbers?

   A. 15
   B. 15.5
   C. 15.75
   D. 16.5
   E. 17.5

13. Critical Thinking

$$3*4 = 12$$
$$2*5 = 30$$
$$4*7 = 84$$
$$5*8 = ??$$

Challenge 46

If $\frac{1}{6}$ of a number is $2\frac{7}{15}$ less than $6\frac{1}{3}$ of that number, $1\frac{4}{5}$ of that number is how much less than 4?

A. $2\frac{4}{15}$

B. $\frac{15}{6}$

C. $\frac{82}{25}$

D. $\frac{33}{15}$

E. $\frac{23}{6}$

[47]

Challenge 47

In 2013, the product of the ages (in integers) of a father and his son is 2013. What is the difference of their ages in 2015?

   A. 20

   B. 24

   C. 28

   D. 30

   E. 32

14. Critical Thinking

What percent of 12 is 12 percent of 1?

Challenge 48

12 years ago Michael was X times as old as Ryan was. If Michael is now 27 years old, how old is Ryan now in terms of X?

A. $\dfrac{15}{X}$

B. $15x$

C. $\dfrac{15}{X} - 12$

D. $\dfrac{15}{X} + 12$

E. $\dfrac{X}{15} + 12$

Challenge 49

John wants to clean his house during this week. He cleaned $\frac{1}{5}$ of his house on Sunday and $\frac{1}{4}$ of the remaining on Monday. On Tuesday, John cleaned $\frac{1}{3}$ of what still remained and $\frac{1}{2}$ of what left on Wednesday. What fraction of the house needs to be cleaned?

A. $\frac{1}{5}$

B. $\frac{1}{6}$

C. $\frac{1}{12}$

D. $\frac{1}{16}$

E. $\frac{1}{24}$

Challenge 50

If 11 workers can build 11 cars in 11 days, then how many days would it take 7 workers to build 7 cars?

    A. 7

    B. 9

    C. 11

    D. 14

    E. 18

Challenge 51

In a sequence of numbers, each term is three less than three times the previous term. If the fourth term in this sequence is 150, what is the first term?

Challenge 52

If 5 workers can build 2 houses in 24 days, then how many days would it take 24 workers to build 10 houses?

A. 10
B. 22
C. 24
D. 25
E. 60

15. Critical Thinking

What is the smallest positive integer p such that $1080p$ is a perfect cube number?

Challenge 53

Nicole bought some marbles. If she had bought four times as many as she did, she would have 33 more. How many marbles did she buy?

Challenge 54

If $9a^2 - b^2 = 11$ and a and b are positive integers, what is the value of a − b?

    A. -5

    B. -3

    C. 3

    D. 5

    E. 7

Challenge 55

Jason's age is $\frac{5}{8}$ of Alice's age now. In ten years, the sum of Jason's and Alice's age will be 72. How old will Alice be in 5 years?

A. 20
B. 30
C. 32
D. 37
E. 42

Challenge 56

Mr. Anderson is 36 years old. His son is 6 years old. After how many years Mr. Anderson's age will become exactly 2.5 times of his son's age?

Challenge 57

The sum of three positive integers is 4000. The ratio of the first number to the second number is $\frac{2}{3}$ and the ratio of the first number to the third number is $\frac{6}{5}$. What is the third number?

   A. 800
   B. 1000
   C. 1200
   D. 1600
   E. 2000

Challenge 58

Three times of Michael's money equals $\frac{2}{3}$ of Jackson's money. If the sum of their money is $2200, how much money does Michael have?

    A. 200

    B. 400

    C. 1000

    D. 1600

    E. 1800

Section Four: Geometry

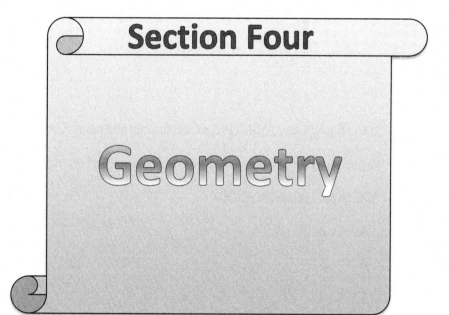

Challenge 59

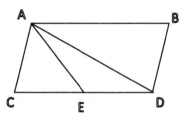

In the figure above, ABCD is a parallelogram and point E is the midpoint of CD. What is the ratio of the area of triangle ADE to parallelogram ABCD?

A. 1:2

B. 1:3

C. 1:4

D. 1:6

E. it cannot be determined

Challenge 60

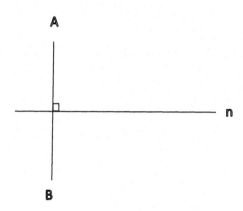

3- In the figure above, A and B are equidistant from the line n. How many circles can be drawn with their centers on line n and that pass through both A and B?

A. 1

B. 2

C. 3

D. 4

E. More than 4

Challenge 61

A solid cube of side 9 is first painted pink and then cut into smaller cubes of side 3. How many of the smaller cubes have paint on exactly 2 sides?

A. 6
B. 8
C. 10
D. 12
E. 16

Challenge 62

The ratio of three sides of a triangle is 1:2:3. What is the smallest angle?

Challenge 63

A rectangle is made of 7 equal squares. If the area of the rectangle is 567 feet, what is the perimeter of the rectangle?

- A. 120 feet
- B. 132 feet
- C. 144 feet
- D. 169 feet
- E. 180 feet

Challenge 64

How many minutes does it take an hour hand of a clock to move 540°?

Challenge 65

If a side of a square is increased by 20%, what percent of the area of the square will be increased?

A. 20%

B. 40%

C. 44%

D. 100%

E. 200%

16. Critical Thinking

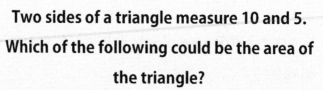

Two sides of a triangle measure 10 and 5. Which of the following could be the area of the triangle?

A) 50 B) 35 C) 25 D) 2 E) 0.1

Challenge 66

What is the degree between the hour hand and minute hand of a clock at 4:30?

17. Critical Thinking

The volume of a cube is one third of the total surface area of the cube. What is the sum of all edges of the cube?

Challenge 67

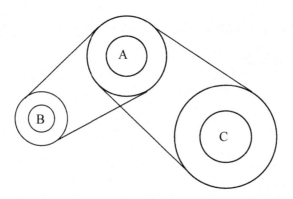

In the figure above, there are three connected wheels. The ratio of the radius of wheel B to the radius of wheel A is 1:3 and the ratio of the radius of wheel A to radius of wheel C is 2:3. When wheel B makes 18 revolutions, how many revolutions does wheel C make?

A. 2
B. 4
C. 8
D. 54
E. 64

[64]

Challenge 68

The sum of three sides of a rectangular is 63. The sum of three sides of the same rectangle is 51. What is the area of the rectangle?

A. 168
B. 169
C. 240
D. 300
E. 325

18. Critical Thinking

The sum of more than two consecutive integers is 17. What is the least number of the integers?

A) 3   B) 16   C) 17   D) 24   E) 34

Challenge 69

A length of a rectangle is increased by 20%. What percent of its width should be decreased to keep the area of the rectangle the same?

A. 15%

B. $16\frac{2}{3}$%

C. 20%

D. 25%

E. 30%

Challenge 70

A cubical block of wood weighs 5 kilograms. How much will another cube of the same wood weigh if its sides are three times as long?

    A. 15

    B. 30

    C. 60

    D. 105

    E. 135

Challenge 71

The total weight of a box and the candies it contains is 12 pounds. After $\frac{2}{3}$ of the candies are eaten, the box and the remaining candies weigh 5 pounds. What is the weight of the empty box in pounds?

A. $\frac{2}{3}$

B. 1

C. $\frac{3}{2}$

D. $2\frac{1}{2}$

E. 5

Challenge 72

The length of a rectangle is three times its width. What is the ratio of its width to its perimeter?

A. 1 : 4
B. 1 : 6
C. 1 : 8
D. 2 : 9
E. 3 : 10

Challenge 73

The perimeter of a square is 13 cm and the perimeter of an equilateral triangle is 7 cm. What is the difference of a side of the square and a side of a triangle?

A. $\frac{7}{13}$ cm

B. $\frac{11}{12}$ cm

C. $1\frac{1}{4}$ cm

D. $2\frac{1}{4}$ cm

E. $\frac{13}{7}$ cm

19. Critical Thinking

N and P are prime numbers. How many divisors $N^2 \times P^4$ has?

Challenge 74

The capacity of a pool is 2100 cubic meters. There is one pope to fill the pool. The pope fills the pool at the rate of 5 cubic meters per 12 minutes. There is a hole at the bottom of the pool and the water exists from the pool at the rate of 3 cubic meters per 45 minutes. How many hours does it take to fill the pool completely?

A. 25
B. 60
C. 85
D. 100
E. 110

Challenge 75

If the total surface area of a cube is 3a square feet and the volume of the cube is 2a cubic feet, then what is the total length, in feet, of all the cube's edges?

A. 12
B. 24
C. 48
D. 64
E. 96

Challenge 76

If the perimeter of an equilateral triangle is 2x meters and its area is x square meters, then what is the length of one side of the triangle in meters?

A. $\sqrt{3}$

B. $\dfrac{\sqrt{3}}{2}$

C. $2\sqrt{3}$

D. $\dfrac{2\sqrt{3}}{3}$

E. 3

Challenge 77

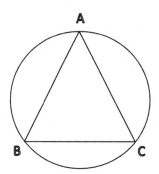

What is the perimeter of the inscribed equilateral triangle, if the diameter of the circle above is 4?

A. $4\sqrt{2}$

B. $4\sqrt{3}$

C. $6\sqrt{2}$

D. $6\sqrt{3}$

E. 12

Section Five: Intelligent Math

Challenge 78

1, 4, 10, 22, 46, A, B

In the series above, A and B represent numbers. What is the value of B?

A. 94
B. 96
C. 122
D. 168
E. 190

Challenge 79

$$\boxed{\dfrac{3}{5}} \to \boxed{\dfrac{11}{19}} \to \boxed{\dfrac{43}{75}} \to \boxed{\dfrac{171}{299}} \to \boxed{?}$$

In the series above, what is the fifth fraction?

A. $\dfrac{191}{480}$

B. $\dfrac{513}{897}$

C. $\dfrac{676}{1199}$

D. $\dfrac{683}{1195}$

E. $\dfrac{689}{1211}$

Challenge 80

What is the 2015th letter of the following pattern?

EFFORTLESSMATHEFFORTLESSMATHEFFORTLESS...

A. A

B. E

C. F

D. O

E. R

F. T

G. L

H. S

Challenge 81

What is the last number in the 18th row in the following pattern?

First row: 2

Second row: 3   4

Third row: 5   6   7

Fourth row: 8   9   10   11

...

A. 169
B. 170
C. 171
D. 172
E. 173

Challenge 82

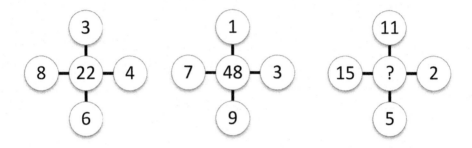

In the figure above, what number should be replaced with a question mark?

Challenge 83

$(-70) + (-60) + (-50) + (-40) + \ldots + n = ?$

If the pattern of the above operation continues, which of the following could be the answer?

A. 90
B. 100
C. 150
D. 170
E. 200

Challenge 84

What is the sum of all fractions?

$$\frac{1}{2}+\frac{1}{4}+\frac{1}{8}+\frac{1}{16}+\ldots+\frac{1}{512}+\frac{1}{1024} = ?$$

20. Critical Thinking

In how many 3 digits number the sum of all digits is 7?

Challenge 85

| 1/7 | ? | ? | 1/6 |

There are 4 fractions in the figure above with the same difference. What is the sum of all fractions?

A. $\dfrac{1}{126}$

B. $\dfrac{7}{33}$

C. $\dfrac{13}{42}$

D. $\dfrac{10}{66}$

E. $\dfrac{13}{21}$

Challenge 86

If $\dfrac{1}{3} = \dfrac{1}{\Delta} + \dfrac{1}{\nabla}$ what is the value of $\nabla \times \Delta$?

Challenge 87

```
      A  B
  +   A  B
  +   A  B
  +   A  B
  ─────────
      C  A
```

In the figure above, A, B and C represent different digits.

What is the value of A + B + C?

A. 9

B. 12

C. 14

D. 18

E. 20

Challenge 88

```
    A  B  C
    A  B  C
+   A  B  C
_____
 D  2  D  C
```

In the figure above, A, B, C, and D represent different digits. What is the value of A × B + C + D?

A. 6
B. 12
C. 34
D. 40
E. 45

[85]

Challenge 89

```
      A  A  A
+     A  A  B
+     A  C  C
   ─────────
   1  3  5  9
```

In the figure above, A, B, and C represent different digits. What is the value of B + C?

A. 8

B. 11

C. 15

D. 17

E. 18

Challenge 90

```
         A   B
    ×    B   A
    ─────────────
         1   0   8
    11   6   0
    ─────────────
    2    2   8   6
```

In the figure above, A and B represent different digits. What is the value of A × B?

A. 8

B. 12

C. 18

D. 24

E. 30

Challenge 91

Mrs. Walters has 61 candles. She burns one candle every day and always makes one new one from the remaining wax of seven burnt candles. After how many days she needs to buy new candles?

   A. 62
   B. 68
   C. 69
   D. 70
   E. 71

Challenge 92

If $\dfrac{1}{B} = \dfrac{1}{A} - \dfrac{1}{20}$ what is the value A + B?

Challenge 93

The numbers in each set of nine numbers are related in a certain way. What is the value of the question mark?

3	8	9	6	5	10
5	11	6	10	6	11
2	7	1	2	5	?

Section Six: Other Topics

Challenge 94

There are 21 students in a class. Their Math teacher asked them this question: "How many of other students in this class have the same name as you?" The teacher asked the students to write their answers in a piece of paper. Then the teacher gathered the answers and removed repeated answers. What is the maximum number of answers that the teacher kept?

A. 0
B. 1
C. 2
D. 20
E. 21

Challenge 95

A book has 500 pages that is numbered from 1 to 500. How many number 2 is used for numbering all pages? (for page 222, three number 2 is used and for 201, one number 2 is used)

A. 100
B. 150
C. 200
D. 210
E. 220

Challenge 96

The date of a Math competition is the third Saturday in May in each year. What is the first possible date of the competition?

- A. 14
- B. 15
- C. 20
- D. 21
- E. 23

Challenge 97

What is the smallest positive integer that has 7 factors?

Challenge 98

In how many ways can Ann, Bea, Cam, Don, Ella and Fey be seated on a straight line if Ann and Bea cannot be seated next to each other?

    A. 240
    B. 360
    C. 480
    D. 620
    E. 720

Challenge 99

Find the highest four-digit number that is divisible by each of the numbers 16, 36, 45 and 80.

Challenge 100

What is the greatest four-digit integer that meets the following three restrictions?

1) All of the digits are different.
2) The greatest digit is the sum of the other three digits.
3) The product of the four digits is divisible by 10 and not equal to zero.

Answers

Challenge 1: C

To answer this question, you can add all the multiples of ten from 110 to 990 and then divide the answer by the number of numbers. As you can imagine, this method takes a lot of time. Another way to solve this problem is by finding the average of the first number 110 and last number 990 (110 + 990 = 1100 ÷ 2 = 550). Do the same thing for the next two numbers 120 and 980. Continue the process for other pair of numbers; 130-970, 140-960, etc. The average of all pairs is 550. Therefore, the average (arithmetic mean) of all the multiples of ten from 110 to 990 inclusive is 550.

Challenge 2: C

Write the numbers in fraction form and simplify:

$$\left(\frac{3}{2}\right) \times \left(\frac{4}{3}\right) \times \left(\frac{5}{4}\right) \times \left(\frac{6}{5}\right) \times \ldots \times \left(\frac{2016}{2015}\right) = \frac{3 \times 4 \times 5 \times 6 \times \ldots \times 2016}{2 \times 3 \times 4 \times 5 \times 6 \times \ldots \times 2015} = \left(\frac{2016}{2}\right) = 1008$$

Challenge 3: B

Write the values of all rectangular and add them.

$$\frac{3}{4}+\frac{9}{4}+\frac{3}{4}+\frac{9}{4}+\frac{3}{4}+\frac{9}{4}+\frac{3}{4}+\frac{9}{4}+\frac{3}{4} = 9\frac{3}{4}$$

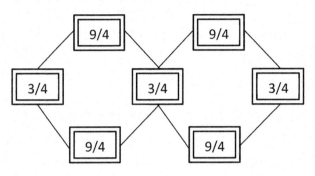

Challenge 4: E

Continue the pattern and add the values of the 7 rectangles in the base of the shape.

3.2 + 18.3 + 43.5 + 55 + 39 + 14.7 + 2.3 = 176

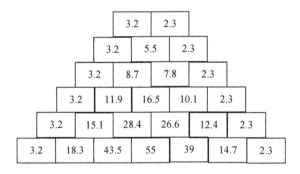

Challenge 5: B

Because there aren't that many perfect squares less than 2016 that is also a perfect cube, let's look for the smallest perfect square number. This happens to be number 1. It is a perfect square number (1 × 1 = 1) and a perfect cube number

(1×1×1=1). To find the next positive perfect square number less than 2015 that is also a perfect cube, let's take a look at number 2. $2^2 = 4$ is a perfect square and $2^3 = 8$ is a perfect cube number and $(2^2)^3 = 2^6 = 64$, which is both a perfect square and cube number. Next perfect square and cube number with the base of 2 is $(2^6)^2 = 2^{12} = 4096$, which is greater than 2016.

With the same method, $3^6 = 729$ is the next perfect square number and cube. $4^6 = 4096$ is a perfect square and cube number, but is bigger than 2016. Therefore, numbers 1, 64 and 729 are the perfect square and cube numbers less than 2016.

Challenge 6: D

There are 33 numbers that are multiple of 3 less than 100 (3, 6, 9, 12, 15, ...) and there are 10 numbers that are ending with 3 (3, 13, 23, 33, 43, ...). From those numbers, 4 numbers (3, 33, 63, 93) are also the multiple of 3. Therefore, there are 39 numbers that are either a multiple of 3 or ending with 3:

33 + 10 − 4 = 39

Challenge 7: B

$a = (5^{11})^2 = 5^{22}$ and $b = 4^{11}$

Change the base of number b from 4 to 2: $b = 2^{22}$

Therefore, $ab = 5^{22} \times 2^{22} = 10^{22}$

Number 10^1 has 2 digits and number 10^2 (100) has 3 digits. Therefore, 10^{22} has 23 digits.

Challenge 8: 25

Each prime number has exactly 2 factors, 1 and the number itself. To find the smallest 2 digits number, n, that has exactly three positive factors, we need to find an odd perfect square number. Why?

The factors of number n are 1, n and a prime number. Let's consider the smallest prime numbers:

2: If 2 is a factor of n, then n should be 4 (1×2×2). This is not the answer. Since, n should be a 2 digits number.

3: If 3 is a factor of n, then n should be 9 (1×3×3). This is not the answer!

5: If 5 is a factor of n, then n should be 25 (1×5×5). Bingo!

Challenge 9: C

We are looking for a number that the sum of its digits equals 5.

Pairs possible: 0,0,0,5; 1,4,0,0; 0,0,2,3; 1,3,1,0; 1,2,1,1; 0,1,2,2

Number of options for each pair:

$0,0,0,5 = \dfrac{4!}{3!} = \dfrac{4 \times 3 \times 2 \times 1}{3 \times 2 \times 1} = 4$ (5, 50, 500, 5,000)

$1,4,0,0 = \dfrac{4!}{2!} = \dfrac{4 \times 3 \times 2 \times 1}{2 \times 1} = 12$ (14, 41, 104, 140, 410, 401, 1004, 1040, 1400, 4001, 4010, 4100)

$0,0,2,3 = \dfrac{4!}{2!} = \dfrac{4 \times 3 \times 2 \times 1}{2 \times 1} = 12$ (23, 32, 230, 320, …)

$1,3,1,0 = \dfrac{4!}{2!} = \dfrac{4 \times 3 \times 2 \times 1}{2 \times 1} = 12$ (113, 131, 311, 1013, …)

$1,2,1,1 = \dfrac{4!}{3!} = \dfrac{4 \times 3 \times 2 \times 1}{3 \times 2 \times 1} = 4$ (1112, 1121, 1211, 2111)

$0,1,2,2 = \dfrac{4!}{2!} = \dfrac{4 \times 3 \times 2 \times 1}{2 \times 1} = 12$ (122, 212, 221, 1022, …)

Total: 12 + 12 + 12 + 12 + 4 + 4 = 56

Challenge 10: D

a=2^{6000}, b=3^{4000} and c=7^{2000}

Find the 2000th rout of each number:

$\sqrt[2000]{a} = \sqrt[2000]{2^{6000}} = 2^{\frac{6000}{2000}} = 2^3 = 8$

$\sqrt[2000]{b} = \sqrt[2000]{3^{4000}} = 3^{\frac{4000}{2000}} = 3^2 = 9$

$\sqrt[2000]{c} = \sqrt[2000]{7^{2000}} = 7^{\frac{2000}{2000}} = 7^1 = 7$

Therefore: c < a < b

Challenge 11: B

Let's consider 1 digit, 2 digits, and 3 digits numbers separately:

One digit number: From 9 1-digit numbers, eight numbers don't have any digit as 5.

Two digits numbers: Put A for 10th place and B for unit place. Then, we have AB as a 2 digits number. We can put 8 digits for A (all digits except 0 and 5) and 9 digits for B (except 5). So, we'll have 8 × 9 = 72 2-digits numbers that don't have 5 as any digits.

For three digits numbers, ABC: For A, we can put 8 digits (not 0 or 5), for B, we have 9 digits (not 5) and for C, we have 9 digits (not 5). So, there are 648 three digits numbers that don't have 5 as any digits. 8 × 9 × 9 = 648

In total: 8 + 72 + 648 = 728

Challenge 12: E

$20^{10} = (2 \times 10)^{10} = 2^{10} \times 10^{10} = 1024 \times 10^{10}$

1024 has four digits and 10^{10} has 11 digits. Why?

Therefore, 20^{10} has 15 digits.

Challenge 13: $3\sqrt{2}$

t and $\sqrt{w}$ are inversely proportional when t = 2 and w=9,

Then, $t \times \sqrt{w} = 2 \times \sqrt{9} = 2 \times 3 = 6$

w =2, then,

$t \times \sqrt{w} = 6 \rightarrow t \times \sqrt{2} = 6 \rightarrow t = \dfrac{6}{\sqrt{2}} \times \dfrac{\sqrt{2}}{\sqrt{2}} = \dfrac{6\sqrt{2}}{2} = 3\sqrt{2}$

Challenge 14: E

$a^x = \dfrac{2}{3} \rightarrow a^{-3x} = \left(\dfrac{2}{3}\right)^{-3} = \dfrac{1}{\left(\dfrac{2}{3}\right)^3} = \dfrac{1}{\dfrac{8}{27}} = \dfrac{27}{8}$

Challenge 15: E

Let's analyze each option:

$2^9 = (2^3)^3$, therefore, 2^9 is a perfect cube number.

$3^8 = (3^4)^2$, therefore, 3^8 is a perfect square number.

$4^7 = (2^2)^7 = 2^{14} = (2^7)^2$, therefore, 4^7 is a perfect square number.

$5^6 = (5^3)^2$, therefore, 5^6 is a perfect square and perfect cube number.

6^5 cannot be written with different base. So, this is the answer!

Challenge 16: D

Try to find the pattern:

$2^1 = 2$, $2^2 = 4$, $2^3 = 8$, $2^4 = 16$, $2^5 = 32$, $2^6 = 64$,

The pattern repeats every 4 numbers. Therefore, when 2^{136} is multiplied out, the unit digit is 6. Why?

Challenge 17: C

Numbers between 500 and 599 begin with 5. So, there are 100 numbers that begin with 5.

Consider numbers that end with 5:

405, 415, 425, 435, ..., 495

Also, numbers 505, 515, 525, ..., 595, end with 5. But, we counted them before!

There are 20 numbers that end with 5. We counted 10 of them before. Therefore, there are 100 + 10 = 110 numbers that begin with digit 5 or end with digit 5.

Challenge 18: E

Factorize 4^{20}:

$4^{20}+4^{20}+4^{20}+4^{20} = 4^{20}(1+1+1+1) = 4^{20}(4) = 4^{21}$

$4^{21} = (2^2)^{21} = 2^{42}$

Challenge 19: $z^{-\frac{4}{3}}$

To find t in terms of z, first we need to find the value of t in terms of p:

$t^{\frac{1}{2}} = p^{\frac{-2}{3}} \rightarrow (t^{\frac{1}{2}})^2 = (p^{\frac{-2}{3}})^2 \rightarrow t = p^{-\frac{4}{9}}$

Now, solve for p

$p^{\frac{1}{6}} = z^{-\frac{1}{2}} \rightarrow \left(p^{\frac{1}{6}}\right)^6 = (z^{-\frac{1}{2}})^6 \rightarrow p = z^{-3} \rightarrow$

$(p)^{-\frac{4}{9}} = (z^{-3})^{-\frac{4}{9}} = z^{-\frac{12}{9}} = z^{-\frac{4}{3}}$

$t = p^{-\frac{4}{9}}$ and $(p)^{-\frac{4}{9}} = z^{-\frac{4}{3}}$, therefore, $t = z^{-\frac{4}{3}}$

Challenge 20: 10

Factorize 2700:

$2700 = 2^2 \times 3^3 \times 5^2$

The product of two perfect cube numbers is another perfect cube number. For example 8 and 27 are perfect cube numbers. The product of 8 and 27 is 216, which is another perfect cube number. (8 × 27 = 216 and 6^3 = 216)

To make *2700m* a perfect cube number we need the product of 5 and 2.

$2700 = 2^2 \times 3^3 \times 5^2$

$2700 \times 10 = 2^3 \times 3^3 \times 5^3$, therefore, m = 10

Challenge 21: B

Divisibility rules for a divisor of 9:

A number is divisible by 9 if the sum of the digits is divisible by 9. For example 126 is divisible by 9, since, 1 + 2 + 6 = 9 is divisible by 9.

$7 \times 10^{83} + 3 = 7,000,...,000 + 3 = 7,000,...,003$

The sum of the digits is 10.

Therefore, the remainder when number 10 is divided by 9 is 1.

Challenge 22: D

$\sqrt[6]{x} = 6 \rightarrow (\sqrt[6]{x})^6 = 6^6 \rightarrow X = 6^6$

$\sqrt{x^6} = \sqrt{(x^6)^6} = \sqrt{x^{36}} = x^{18}$

Challenge 23: E

$(2^{89} - 2^{88})(2^{77} - 2^{76}) = ?$

Factorize common factors:

$2^{88}(2-1) \times 2^{76}(2-1) = 2^{88} \times 2^{76} = 2^{164}$

Challenge 24: B

Put x for the number of current girls and y for the number of current boys at the school. First, let's set up our ratios.

$\dfrac{x}{y} = \dfrac{2}{7}$ and $\dfrac{x+10}{y} = \dfrac{3}{8}$

Use cross multiplication to write the equations.

$7x = 2y$ and $8(x+10) = 3y \Rightarrow 8x + 80 = 3y$

Now, we have a system of equations with two variables.

$7x - 2y = 0$ $\qquad\qquad\qquad\qquad$ $21x - 6y = 0$

$8x - 3y = -80$ $\qquad\qquad\qquad\quad$ $-16x + 6y = 160$

From the system of equations above: x = 32 and y = 112

32 girls are currently attending the school.

Challenge 25: B

The total amount of the mixture of two fuels is 60 liters. (20 liter plus 40 liters) Let's find the total of the antifreeze.

The sum of 40 % of 20 liters and 10% of 40 liters is:

0.40 × 20 + 0.10 × 40 = 8 + 4 = 12

Of 60 liters of the mixture, 12 liters are antifreeze. So, the percentage of antifreeze in the new solution is:

12 ÷ 60 = 0.20 = 20%

Challenge 26: 400

Let's choose x for the original price of the computer. Then,

0.80 x = 0.85 x − 20 → 0.05x = 20 → x = 400

The original price of the computer is $400

Challenge 27: D

The ratio of sugar to flour is $\frac{1}{2}$ to 2. Therefore, the ratio of the flour to whole is 2 to $2\frac{1}{2}$ or $\frac{2}{2\frac{1}{2}}$ = 0.8 = 80%

Therefore, 80% of the cake is flour.

Challenge 28: C

Choose x for current price of the car. In the first year, the price of the car reduced to 0.90 x. Next year, it'll be

0.90x × 0.80 = 0.72x.

For the third year, the price of the car is: 0.72x × 0.75 = 0.54 x

Therefore, 46% of the original price is the total reduction of the car's price.

Challenge 29: D

The ratio of men to women is 3 to 5 and the ratio of women to children is 2 to 7. First, let's find the ratio of men to women to children. The ratio of 3 to 5 equals the ratio of 6 to 10. The ratio of 2 to 7 is the same as the ratio of 10 to 35.

Therefore, the ratio of men to women to children is 6: 10: 35.

Now, you can find the ratio of men and women to children.

6 + 10 to 35 or 16: 35.

Challenge 30: C

Let x be the first number and y the next number. Therefore:

xy = 216 and x + y = 35. Solve the second equation for x:

x + y = 35 → x = 35 − y

Replace the value of x in the second equation with x in the first equation.

xy = 216 → (35 − y) y = 216 → 35y − y² = 216 →

$y^2 - 35y + 216 = 0$

Factorize the polynomial: $(y - 8)(y - 27) = 0$

$y = 8$ or $y = 27$

The difference is 19.

Challenge 31: C

Sophia has 6 lessons in two weeks and Lukas has one lesson in two weeks. Therefore, the difference is 5 lessons for two weeks or 2.5 lessons per week. The difference is 40 lessons. So, $40 \div 2.5 = 16$

Their term is 16 weeks.

Challenge 32: D

Keep in mind that the number of workers and the number of days are inversely proportional. It means that with more workers, it takes less time to build a house.

First, find the constant. W (number of workers) × D (days) = 8 × 20 = 160

Then, W × 4 (days) = 160 → W = 40

40 workers are needed to build the house in 4 days!

Challenge 33: C

Let A be Alex's age and R be Ron's age. The ratio of their ages is 3 to 5 and the difference between their ages is 12 years. Therefore, $R = A + 12$ and $A = \frac{3}{5}R$

Replace A in the first equation with its value in the second equation.

$R = A + 12 \rightarrow R = \frac{3}{5}R + 12 \rightarrow \frac{2}{5}R = 12 \rightarrow R = 30$ and $A = 18$

The sum of their ages is 48.

Challenge 34: A

Let J be Janet's money, E be Elliot's money, and S be Sarah's money. Therefore,

$J + E + S = 464$

$J = \frac{2}{3}E \rightarrow E = \frac{3}{2}J$ and $S = \frac{2}{5}J$

Replace the value of E and S in the first equation with their values in the second and third equations:

$J + \frac{3}{2}J + \frac{2}{5}J = 464 \rightarrow 1\frac{19}{10}J = 464 \rightarrow J = 160$

Janet received $160!

Challenge 35: 18

Let E be the age of Eric, T be the age of Tara and M be the age of Marshall.

$E + T + M = 66$

The ratio of E to T is 2 to 3. So:

$$E = \frac{2}{3}T$$

The ratio of T to M is 9 to 7. So:

$$M = \frac{7}{9}T$$

Replace the value of E and M in the first equation with their values in the second and third equations:

$$\frac{2}{3}T + T + \frac{7}{9}T = 66 \rightarrow \frac{22}{9}T = 66 \rightarrow T = 27$$

$$E = \frac{2}{3}T \Rightarrow E = \frac{2}{3}(27) = 18$$

Eric is 18 years old now.

Challenge 36: E

Let H represents the number of seeds a hen eats each day, C represents the number of seeds a chicken eats each day and R represents the number of seeds a rooster eats each day. Therefore,

H + C + R = 4205

H = 2.5 C and R = 1.5 H → R = 1.5 (2.5 C) → R = 3.75 C

Replace the value of H and R in the first equation with their values in the second and third equations:

2.5 C + C + 3.75 C = 4205 → 7.25 C = 4205 → C = 580

H = 2.5 C → H = 2.5 (580) = 1450

A hen eats 1450 seeds in one day.

Challenge 37: B

Let x be the Alice's money. Then: $\frac{2}{5}x$ = $15 + $15 = $30

X = $75

After buying two books, Alice has $45. $\frac{2}{9}$ of $45 is $10.

10 ÷ 4 = 2.5

The price of each pencil was $2.50

Challenge 38: E

200 % of a half of $\frac{1}{5}$ of a tank equals to $\frac{1}{5}$ of the tank!

Half of $\frac{1}{5}$ equals to $\frac{1}{10}$. 200 % of $\frac{1}{10}$ equals to $\frac{1}{5}$.

90 gallons of gas fills the difference of $\frac{1}{5}$ and half ($\frac{1}{2}$) of the tank. Therefore:

$\frac{1}{2}T - \frac{1}{5}T = 90 \rightarrow \frac{3}{10}T = 90 \rightarrow T = 300$

Challenge 39: B

5 hours = 300 minutes. Use the formula: $\frac{1}{a} + \frac{1}{b} = \frac{1}{t}$

Where, a is the rate for the first person and b is the rate of the second person. Joe can finish the job in 5 hours (300 minutes) and they both can finish the job in 100 minutes.

$\frac{1}{300} + \frac{1}{b} = \frac{1}{100} \rightarrow \frac{1}{b} = \frac{1}{100} - \frac{1}{300} \rightarrow b = 150$

150 minutes takes Mark to finish the job

Challenge 40: B

Let X, Y and Z represent the three numbers. Therefore:

$X + Y = \frac{11}{5}$, $Y + Z = \frac{31}{15}$, $X + Z = \frac{31}{15}$

Add the three questions:

$(X + Y) + (Y + Z) + (X + Z) = \frac{11}{5} + \frac{31}{15} + \frac{7}{3}$

$2X + 2Y + 2Z = \frac{99}{15} \to 2(X + Y + Z) = \frac{99}{15} \to X + Y + Z = \frac{99}{30} = \frac{33}{10}$

The average of the three numbers is:

$\frac{X + Y + Z}{3} = \frac{33}{10} \div 3 = \frac{33}{30} = 1\frac{1}{10}$

Challenge 41: E

Let A be the price of the apple. Therefore:

$2A = 5A - 2.55 \to 3A = 2.55 \to A = 0.85$

The price of 4 pounds of apple is:

$4 \times 0.85 = 3.4$

Challenge 42: 13

Mr. Ronald is 53 years old and the sum of his children is:

$14 + 9 + 4 = 27$

The difference of Mr. Ronald's age and his children is:

$53 - 27 = 26$

Every year, one year adds to Mr. Ronald's age and three years adds to the sum of his children's age. The difference of this is 2 years. So, each year 2 years is subtracted from the difference of Mr. Ronal's age and his children.

Therefore, in 13 years the difference of Mr. Ronald's age and his children becomes zero.

Challenge 43: B

Peter is 35% faster than David. Therefore, when David finishes a job, Peter finishes 1.35 of the same job.

Let's assume that David prepares 54 units in 54 days. Then, Peter can prepares 54 × 1.35 = 72.9 units in the same time.

Now, how long does it take Peter to prepare 54 units?

$$\frac{54}{x} = \frac{72.9}{54} \Rightarrow x = 40$$

It takes Peter 40 days to finish the same job.

Challenge 44: B

Edward can finish 40% of a job in 2 days. Therefore, he can finish the job in 5 days.

40% of x = 2 → x = 5

Emanuel can finish 15% of the same job in 3 days. So, he can finish the whole job in 20 days.

15% of x = 3 → x = 20

First, let's find the time it takes to finish the job if both Edward and Emanuel work together.

$$\frac{1}{a} + \frac{1}{b} = \frac{1}{t} \rightarrow \frac{1}{5} + \frac{1}{20} = \frac{1}{t} \rightarrow \frac{5}{20} = \frac{1}{t} \rightarrow t = 4$$

It takes 4 days to finish the job if both of them work together. Therefore, they can finish 75% of the job in 3 days:

x = 4 → 75% of x equals 3.

Challenge 45: C

The average of 14 numbers is 18. Therefore, the sum of 14 numbers is 252.

The average of 18 numbers is 14. Therefore, the sum of 18 numbers is 252. The sum of all 32 numbers is 504.

The average of 32 numbers is: 504 ÷ 32 = 15.75

Challenge 46: C

Let x be the number. Then:

$$\frac{1}{6}x = 6\frac{1}{3}x - 2\frac{7}{15} \Rightarrow 6\frac{1}{3}x - \frac{1}{6}x = 2\frac{7}{15} \Rightarrow \frac{37}{6}x = \frac{37}{15}$$

$$X = \frac{2}{5}$$

Then:

$$1\frac{4}{5}x = \frac{9}{5} \times \frac{2}{5} = \frac{18}{25}$$

$$4 - \left(\frac{18}{25}\right) = 3\frac{7}{25} = \frac{82}{25}$$

Challenge 47: C

Find the factors of 2013:

1, 3, 11, 33, 61, 671, 2013

From all the factors of 2013, only 33 and 61 could be the ages of a father and his son. (The product of two ages should be 2013)

The difference of 61 and 33 is 28 years and this number won't change in 2015!

Challenge 48: D

12 years ago Michael was 15 years old. At that time, he was X times as old as Ryan was. Plug is a value for X. Let's say X is 3. Therefore, Ryan was 5 years old 12 years ago. Now, Ryan is 17.

Plug in 3 for X and check all 5 options:

A. $\frac{15}{3} = 3$, B. $15 \times 3 = 45$, C. $\frac{15}{3} - 12 = -7$,

D. $\frac{15}{3} + 12 = 17$! Bingo

E. $\frac{3}{15} + 12 = 12\frac{3}{15}$

Challenge 49: A

John cleaned $\frac{1}{5}$ of his house on Sunday and $\frac{1}{4}$ of the remaining on Monday.

The remaining on Monday was $\frac{4}{5}$. Therefore, $\frac{1}{4}$ of $\frac{4}{5}$ equals:

$\frac{1}{4} \times \frac{4}{5} = \frac{4}{20} = \frac{1}{5}$. So, he cleaned $\frac{1}{5}$ of his house on Sunday and another $\frac{1}{5}$ of his house on Monday. The remaining for the next day is $\frac{3}{5}$ of the house.

On Tuesday, John cleaned $\frac{1}{3}$ of what still remained. $\frac{1}{3}$ of $\frac{3}{5}$ of the house equals:

$\frac{1}{3} \times \frac{3}{5} = \frac{3}{15} = \frac{1}{5}$. So far, he has cleaned $\frac{3}{5}$ of the house and $\frac{2}{5}$ of the house is left.

He cleaned $\frac{1}{2}$ of what left ($\frac{2}{5}$ of the house) on Wednesday. $\frac{1}{2}$ of $\frac{2}{5}$ of the house equals:

$\frac{1}{2} \times \frac{2}{5} = \frac{2}{10} = \frac{1}{5}$.

Therefore, $\frac{1}{2}$ of the house needs to be cleaned.

Challenge 50: A

If 11 workers can build 11 cars in 11 days, then 11 workers can build one car per day. (Find the rate of cars per day)

If, 11 workers can build one car per day, then, one worker can make a car in 11 days. (Each worker can build $\frac{1}{11}$ of a car per day. So, it takes 11 days for a worker to make a car)

If one worker can make a car in 11 days, then it takes 77 days for a worker to make 7 cars. With this rate, 7 workers can make 7 cars in 11 days. Why?

Challenge 51: 7

Each term is three less than three times the previous term. If the fourth term is 150, therefore, the third term is 51.

The second term is 18. Because, 51 is 3 less than 54, which is three time of 18.

The first term is 7!

Challenge 52: D

If 5 workers can build 2 houses in 24 days, they can make 1 house in 12 days. Therefore, each worker can make one house in 60 days. (5 × 12 = 60)

One worker can make 10 houses in 600 days. Therefore, 24 workers can make 10 houses in 25 days. (600 ÷ 24 = 25)

Challenge 53: 11

Let x be the number of marbles Nicole bought. Then:

4x = x + 33 → x = 11

Nicole bought 11 marbles. If she had bought four times as many as she did (4 × 11 = 44), she would have 33 more marbles.

(11 + 33 = 44)

Challenge 54: B

Factorize $9a^2 - b^2$ and 11

$(3a - b)(3a + b) = 11 \times 1$

Therefore, $3a - b$ equals to 11 or 1 and $3a + b$ equals to 1 or 11.

Let's check both:

$3a - b = 1$ and $3a + b = 11$

Solve the above system of equation:

$a = 2$ and $b = 5$

$3a - b = 11$ and $3a + b = 1$

$a = 2$ and $b = -5$

Since, a and b are positive integers, then, only $a = 2$ and $b = 5$ are the solutions.

Therefore, $a - b = 2 - 5 = -3$

Challenge 55: D

Let J be the Jason's age and A be the Alice's age. Then:

$J = \frac{5}{8} A$

In 10 years: $(J + 10) + (A + 10) = 72$

Replace J with its value in the first equation:

Then: $(\frac{5}{8} A + 10) + (A + 10) = 72 \rightarrow 1\frac{5}{8} A = 52 \rightarrow A = 32$

In 5 years, Alice will be 37. (32 + 5 = 37)

Challenge 56: 14

Let x be the number of years that Mr. Anderson's age will become 2.5 times of his son's age. Therefore:

36 + x = 2.5 (6 + x) → 36 + x = 15 +2.5 x → 21 = 1.5x → x = 14

In 14 years, Mr. Anderson will be 50 years, (36 + 14 = 50) which is 2.5 times of his son who will be 20 years.

Challenge 57: B

Let X, Y and Z represent the three numbers. So,

X + Y + Z = 4000 and

$X = \frac{2}{3}Y \rightarrow Y = \frac{3}{2}X$

$X = \frac{6}{5}Z \rightarrow Z = \frac{5}{6}X$

Replace the values of Y and Z in the first equations with their values in the second and third equations:

$X + \frac{3}{2}X + \frac{5}{6}X = 4000 \rightarrow X = 1200$

$Y = \frac{3}{2}X \rightarrow Y = \frac{3}{2}(1200) = 1800$

$Z = \frac{5}{6}X \rightarrow Z = \frac{5}{6}(1200) = 1000$

The third number, Z, is 1000.

Challenge 58: B

Let M be Michael's money and J be Jackson's money. Therefore:

M + J = 2200 and $3M = \frac{2}{3}J \rightarrow M = \frac{2}{9}J$

Replace the value of M in the first equation with its value in the second equation.

$\frac{2}{9}J + J = 2200 \rightarrow J = 1800$

$M = \frac{2}{9}J \rightarrow M = \frac{2}{9}(1800) = 400$

Michael has $400.

Challenge 59: C

AD divides the parallelogram in half. AE divides the half parallelogram into half again. Because the heights of triangles ACE and ADE are equal and their bases are equal. Triangle ADE is, therefore, one fourth of the parallelogram. And the ratio is 1 : 4

Challenge 60: E

Since, the distance from any point on line n to the points A and B are equal, then, any point on line n can be the center of a circle. The distance from that point to either A or B could be the radius of a circle.

Challenge 61: D

Drawing a diagram can help you find the number of small cubes that have paint on exactly 2 sides. When the larger cube is cut into smaller cubes, the cubes in the middle of the faces will have paint on only one side and the corner cubes will have paint on three sides. The cubes cut from the edges will have paint on two sides. Since there are 12 edges, there will be 12 cubes with paint on two sides.

Challenge 62: 30 degree

There is the same ratio for the angels. Therefore, the ratio of three angles of the triangle is also 1:2:3.

Let X be the smallest angle. Then, the next two angels are 2X and 3X.

$X + 2X + 3X = 180 \rightarrow 6X = 180 \rightarrow X = 30$

The smallest angel is 30 degree.

Challenge 63: C

The rectangle is made of 7 equal squares. Therefore, the ratio of the width and length of the rectangle is 1 to 7. Why?

Let X be the width of the rectangle. So,

$X \times 7X = 567 \rightarrow 7X^2 = 567 \rightarrow X^2 = 81 \rightarrow X = 9$

The width of the rectangle is 9 feet and the length is 63 feet.

$(7 \times 9 = 63)$

The perimeter of the rectangle is:

2 × (9 + 63) = 144 feet

Challenge 64: 1080 minutes

A clock has 12 sections from 1 to 12. An hour hand of a clock moves 30 degree in one hour.

360 ÷ 12 = 30

540 ÷ 30 = 18

It takes 18 hours (or 18 × 60 = 1080 minutes) an hour hand of a clock to move 540°.

Challenge 65: C

Area of a square = side times side.

Let X be the side of a square. Then, the side of the square is X^2.

If a side of a square is increased by 20%, then the area of the square will be increased by 44 percent:

1.2X × 1.2X = 1.44X^2

1.44X^2 is 0.44 or 44% bigger than X^2.

Challenge 66: 45 degree

From question 64 we learned that an hour hand of a clock moves 30 degree in one hour. At 4:30, the hour hand of the clock has moved 135 degree. (4.5 × 30 = 135)

At 4:30, the minute hand has moved 180 degree. So, the angle between hour and minute hand of the clock equals:

180 − 135 = 45 degree

Challenge 67: B

Since, the three wheels are connected; we need to find the ratio of the circumference of all wheels:

The circumference of a circle = $2\pi r$

The ratio of the radius of wheel B to wheel A is 1 to 3. Let r_A be the radius of the wheel A and r_B be the radius of the wheel B. Then:

$r_A = 3r_B$

Circumference of the wheel A = $2\pi\, r_A$

Replace r_A with r_B. Then:

Circumference of the wheel A = $2\pi\, r_A = 2\pi\, (3r_B) = 6\pi\, r_B$

The ratio of the circumference of wheel B to A is:

$2\pi\, r_B : 2\pi\, r_A \rightarrow 2\pi\, r_B : 6\pi\, r_B \rightarrow 2 : 6 \rightarrow 1 : 3$

Therefore, the ratio of the circumference of wheel B to A is 1 to 3. (Similar to their radius)

With the same method, the ratio of the circumference of the wheel A to C is 2 to 3.

Therefore, the ratio of the wheels B, A and C is:

B : A = 1 : 3 = 2 : 6

A : C = 2 : 3 = 6 : 9 → B : A : C = 2 : 6 : 9

The ratio of the circumference of the wheel B to the wheel C is 2 to 9 or:

The circumference of the wheel B = $\frac{2}{9}$ the circumference of the wheel C.

B = 18 → C = 18 $(\frac{2}{9})$ = 4

When wheel B makes 18 revolutions, wheel C makes 4 revolutions.

Challenge 68: E

A rectangle has two widths and two lengths. Therefore, the perimeter equals: 2 × (width + length)

Since, the sum of three sides of a rectangular is 63 and the sum of other three sides of the rectangle is 51. Let's assume the width is smaller the length. Let W be the width and L be the length. Therefore:

2W + L = 51 and W + 2 L = 63

Solve the system of equations:

2W + L = 51 → L = 51 – 2W

W + 2 L = 63 → W + 2 (51 – 2W) = 63 → W + 102 – 4W = 63 →

W = 13 and W + 2 L = 63 → 13 + 2L = 63 → 2L = 50 → L = 25

The area of the rectangle is:

W × L = 13 × 25 = 325

Challenge 69: B

The area of a rectangle is the product of its width and length. Let x be the area of the rectangle.

Area of a rectangle = Width × Length = x

Length → 1.2Length → Area of a rectangle = Width × 1.2Length = x

Let W1 be the width of the first rectangle and W2 be the width of the second rectangle.

W1 × 1.2L = W2 × L → W1 × 1.2 = W2 → W1 = $\frac{1}{1.2}$W2 →

W1 = $\frac{5}{6}$ W2

To keep the area of the rectangle the same $\frac{1}{6}$ or $16\frac{2}{3}$ percent of the width should be decreased.

Challenge 70: E

Weight is proportional to volume.

Volume of a cube = (one side)^3

Let x be the side of the first cube. So:

Volume = x^3

The sides of the second cube are three times as long. So:

Volume = $(3x)^3 = 27x^3$

The ratio of the volumes of the old and new cubes will be 1: 27. So, if the first weighs 5 kilograms, the second weighs 27 × 5 kilograms =135 kilogram.

Challenge 71: C

Let "B" be the weight of the box and "C" be the weight of the candies. So:

B + C = 12

After $\frac{2}{3}$ of the candies are eaten, the box and the remaining candies weigh 5 pounds. So,

$B + \frac{1}{3}C = 5$

Solve the system of two equations:

B + C = 12 → B = 12 – C

$B + \frac{1}{3}C = 5 \rightarrow 12 - C + \frac{1}{3}C = 5 \rightarrow 12 - \frac{2}{3}C = 5 \rightarrow C = 10.5$

B = 12 – C → B = 12 – 10.5 = 1.5

The weight of the box is 1.5 pounds.

Challenge 72: C

Let x be the width of the rectangle. So, the length of the rectangle is 3x.

Perimeter of a rectangle = 2 × Width + 2 × Length =

2x + 2 (3x) = 8x

The ratio of its width to its perimeter is 1 to 8.

Challenge 73: B

The perimeter of a square is 13cm. Therefore, one side of the square is $\frac{13}{4}$cm.

The perimeter of the equilateral triangle is 7cm. Therefore, one side of the triangle is $\frac{7}{3}$cm.

The difference of a side of the square and a side of a triangle is:

$$\frac{13}{4} - \frac{7}{3} = \frac{39-28}{12} = \frac{11}{12} \text{ cm}$$

Challenge 74: D

The pope fills the pool at the rate of 5 cubic meters per 12 minutes. So, the rate of filling the pool per hour is 5 × 5 = 25 cubic meters.

The water exists from the pool at the rate of 3 cubic meters per 45 minutes or 4 cubic meters per hour. Therefore, the pool will be filled at the rate of 25 cubic meters − 4 cubic meters = 21 cubic meters.

The capacity of a pool is 2100 cubic meters. So, it takes 100 hours (2100 ÷ 21 = 100) to fill the pool completely.

Challenge 75: C

A cube has 12 edges. Let x be the edge of the cube. So:

Surface area of the cube = 6 (one side)^2 = 6x^2 =3a

$x^2 = \frac{1}{2}a \rightarrow x = \sqrt{\frac{1}{2}a} = (\frac{1}{2}a)^{1/2}$

Volume of the cube = (one side)^3 = x^3 = 2a $\rightarrow$ x = $\sqrt[3]{2a}$ = $(2a)^{1/3}$

Solve for a for both equations:

$(\frac{1}{2}a)^{1/2} = (2a)^{1/3}$

Both sides to the power of 6:

$(\frac{1}{2}a)^3 = (2a)^2 \rightarrow \frac{1}{8}a^3 = 4a^2$

$\rightarrow \frac{1}{8}a = 4 \rightarrow a = 32$

Therefore, the volume of the cube is 64 cubic feet and one side is 4.

The total length of all the cube's edges is 48 feet. (4 × 12 = 48)

Challenge 76: C

The perimeter of the equilateral triangle is 2x meters. So, one side is $\frac{2}{3}$x meters.

The area of an equilateral triangle = $\frac{s^2\sqrt{3}}{4}$ (s is one side of the triangle)

The perimeter of the triangle is twice its area. So:

$2x = 2(\frac{s^2\sqrt{3}}{4}) \rightarrow 2x = (\frac{s^2\sqrt{3}}{2})$

Replace the s with $\frac{2}{3}x$. Then:

$$2x = \frac{(\frac{2}{3}x)^2 \sqrt{3}}{2} = \frac{\frac{4}{9}x^2\sqrt{3}}{2} \to 4x = \frac{4}{9}x^2\sqrt{3} \to 4 = \frac{4}{9}x\sqrt{3} \to 9 = x\sqrt{3} \to$$

$$\frac{9}{\sqrt{3}} = x \to \frac{9}{\sqrt{3}} \times \frac{\sqrt{3}}{\sqrt{3}} = x \to x = 3\sqrt{3}$$

Then, one side of the triangle is: $\frac{2}{3}x = \frac{2}{3}(3\sqrt{3}) = 2\sqrt{3}$

Challenge 77: D

Draw the bisector of the angle A perpendicular to line BC.

D is the center of the circle and CD is equal to the radius. The diameter of the circle above is 4. So, CD is 2.

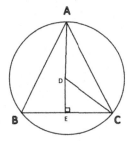

Triangle CDE is a 30-60-90 degree triangle and angle DCE is 30.

Since, CD is 2 (the hypotenuse of the triangle CDE), DE is 1 and CE is $\sqrt{3}$. Why?

Therefore, BC is $2\sqrt{3}$ and the perimeter of the triangle ABC is

$3 \times 2\sqrt{3} = 6\sqrt{3}$

Challenge 78: E

To the value of B, you should find the pattern of the numbers.

The difference of the first number, 1, and second number, 4, is 3. The difference of 4 and 10 is 6. The difference of 10 and 22 is 12 and the difference of 22 and 46 is 24.

The differences are:

3, 6, 12, 24,

Therefore, the difference of each item is twice the difference of the previous item and the number before that. So, the difference of number A and 46 is 48.

A = 46 + 48 = 94

The difference of B and 94 is 96 (2 × 48).

B = 94 + 96 = 190

Challenge 79: D

Find the pattern in the number series. Each numerator or denominator of the fraction is one less than four times the previous numerator or denominator.

3 → 11

3 (4) − 1 = 11

171 × 4 − 1 = 683

299 × 4 − 1 = 1195

The number fraction is:

$\boxed{\dfrac{3}{5}} \rightarrow \boxed{\dfrac{11}{19}} \rightarrow \boxed{\dfrac{43}{75}} \rightarrow \boxed{\dfrac{171}{299}} \rightarrow \boxed{\dfrac{683}{1195}}$

Challenge 80: F

In EFFORTLESSMATH, the pattern repeats after every 14 letters.

2015 is not divisible by 14. So, find the smaller number less than 2015 that is divisible by 14. That number is 2002.

2015 − 2002 = 13. The 13th letter is T.

Challenge 81: D

Each row has one number more than the previous row. The first row has one number, the second row has two numbers, and the 18th row has 18 numbers.

To answer the question, we should find the number of numbers in all 18 rows.

$1 + 2 + 3 + \ldots + 17 + 18 = \dfrac{18}{2}(1+18) = 171$

The first number starts with 2. Therefore, the last number is 172 (171 +1).

Challenge 82: 162

To find the answer, you need to find the pattern. The number in the center is the product of the number on the left and the above number minus the difference of the two other numbers.

The number in the center on the right is:

(15 × 11) − (5 − 2) = 162

Challenge 83: D

The first number in the equation is -70 and the next item is 10 more than the previous number. If the pattern continues, the sum of all numbers till number +70 is 0. Why?

The next number is 80 and the number after that is 90.

80 + 90 = 170

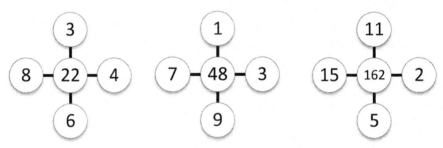

Challenge 84: $\frac{1023}{1024}$

$$\frac{1}{2} + \frac{1}{4} + \frac{1}{8} + \frac{1}{16} + \ldots + \frac{1}{512} + \frac{1}{1024} =$$

To add the fractions, we need to find the common denominator.

The common denominator is 1024. Therefore:

$$\frac{512}{1024} + \frac{256}{1024} + \frac{128}{1024} + \ldots + \frac{2}{1024} + \frac{1}{1024} =$$

$$\frac{512 + 256 + 128 + 64 + 32 + 16 + 8 + 4 + 2 + 1}{1024} = \frac{1023}{1024}$$

Challenge 85: E

| $\frac{1}{7}$ | ? | ? | $\frac{1}{6}$ |

There are four fractions with the same difference. First, we need to find the missing fractions.

The difference of $\frac{1}{7}$ and $\frac{1}{6}$ is:

$$\frac{1}{6} - \frac{1}{7} = \frac{7-6}{42} = \frac{1}{42}$$

The difference of $\frac{1}{7}$ and the first fraction is:

$$\frac{1}{42} \div 3 = \frac{1}{126}$$

The first missing fraction is:

$$\frac{1}{7} + \frac{1}{126} = \frac{18+1}{126} = \frac{19}{126}$$

The second missing fraction is:

$$\frac{19}{126} + \frac{1}{126} = \frac{20}{126}$$

The sum of all fractions equals:

$$\frac{1}{7} + \frac{19}{126} + \frac{20}{126} + \frac{1}{6} = \frac{18}{126} + \frac{19}{126} + \frac{20}{126} + \frac{21}{126} = \frac{78}{126} = \frac{13}{21}$$

Challenge 86: 48

∇ and Δ are two digits. The sum of two fractions $\frac{1}{\Delta}$ and $\frac{1}{\nabla}$ equals to $\frac{1}{3}$. Obviously, there are many values for ∇ and Δ that can be used in the equation.

Choose a value for ∇. Let's put 4 for ∇. Then:

$\frac{1}{3} = \frac{1}{\Delta} + \frac{1}{4} \rightarrow \frac{1}{3} - \frac{1}{4} = \frac{1}{\Delta} \rightarrow \frac{4}{12} - \frac{3}{12} = \frac{1}{\Delta} \rightarrow \frac{1}{12} = \frac{1}{\Delta} \rightarrow \Delta = 12$

Therefore: $\nabla \times \Delta = 4 \times 12 = 48$

Challenge 87: C

A, B and C represent different digits. Plug in different digits for B and find the value of A. Remember that the sum of four 2-digit numbers is another 2-digit number. Therefore, the value of A cannot be more than 2. Why?

A is 1 or 2. The value of 1 for A is not possible. Because the sum of four same numbers (B) cannot be 1, 11 or 21, and 31.

A is 2. So, B can be 3 or 8.

B cannot be 8. Because 4 times 28 is 112, which is not a 2-digit number.

B is 3. Then, C is 9.

A + B + C = 2 + 3 + 9 = 14

Challenge 88: 6

A, B, C, and D represent different digits. The sum of three 3-digit numbers is a 4-digit number with 1 or 2 in the thousands place. Therefore, D = 1 or 2. And A is 3 or greater than 3. Why?

A + A + A = 12 or 12+1, Why?

Since, A is a digit, then 3A cannot be 13. 3A = 12 ⇒ A = 4

We also know that C + C + C = C or C + 10

C = 0 or 3C = C + 10 → 2C = 10 → C = 5

Therefore, C is 0 or 5.

Let's assume D = 1. Then:

If C = 0 → B + B + B = 1 or B + B + B = 1 + 10

3B = 1 (This is not correct) or 3B = 1 + 10 (This is not correct either).

If C = 5 → B + B + B + 1 = D → D = 1 → 3B = 1 – 1= 0

or

B + B + B + 1 = D + 10 → 3B + 1 = 1 + 10 → B = $\frac{10}{3}$

B is an integer and cannot be $\frac{10}{3}$.

In this situation, the only value of B is 0.

If A = 4, B = 0 and C = 5, then 405 + 405 + 405 = 1215 Bingo!

You can check out other values for A, B, C, and D. But, only the above values work.

A × B + C + D = 4 × 0 + 5 + 1 = 6

Challenge 89: C

In this problem, we can write a system of three equations and three variables.

Let's review the equations.

A + B + C = 9 or 19

A + A + C = 5 or 15

A + A + A = 13 or 12

3A cannot be 13. Therefore, 3A = 12 ⟹ A = 4

We can also conclude that in the second equation:

A + A + C = 15 ⟹ 2A + C = 15 ⟹ C = 7

Or A + A + C = 16 (1 may added from the first column)

C = 6

Try different values for the first equation:

A + B + C = 9 or 19

If A = 4 and C = 6 ⟹ B = 9

If A = 4 and C = 7 ⟹ B = 8

B + C = 15

Challenge 90: D

A and B represent different digits and A × AB = 108

Therefore, A = 3? Why?

3 × 3B = 108 ⇒ B = 8

Then: A × B = 3 × 8 = 24

Challenge 91: E

Mrs. Walters burns one candle every day and she can make a new one from the remaining wax of seven burnt candles. After 56 days, Mrs. Walters can make 8 new candles. (56 ÷ 7 = 8)

So, she has 13 candles now. After seven days, she burns 7 candles and makes another candle. So, she has 7 candles now. She can burn these 7 candles in 7 days and make a new candle after that for another day.

Therefore, she needs to buy new candles after 71 days:

56 + 7 + 7 + 1 = 71

Challenge 92: 9

$$\frac{1}{B} = \frac{1}{A} - \frac{1}{20}$$

Therefore, A is less than B. Why?

Plug in different values for A.

Let's begin with 2. If $A = 2 \rightarrow \frac{1}{B} = \frac{1}{2} - \frac{1}{20} \rightarrow \frac{1}{B} = \frac{9}{20} \rightarrow 9B = 20$

B is an integer. Therefore, B cannot be $\frac{20}{9}$

$A = 3 \rightarrow \frac{1}{B} = \frac{1}{3} - \frac{1}{20} \rightarrow \frac{1}{B} = \frac{17}{60} \rightarrow 17B = 60$

$A = 4 \rightarrow \frac{1}{B} = \frac{1}{4} - \frac{1}{20} \rightarrow \frac{1}{B} = \frac{4}{20} \rightarrow 4B = 20 \rightarrow B = 5$ Bingo!

$A = 4$ and $B = 5 \rightarrow A + B = 9$

Challenge 93: 1

Column 3 on right is the sum of two columns of the right set minus the difference of the two right columns of the left set of numbers.

3	8	9		6	5	11-1
5	11	6		10	6	16-5
2	7	1		2	5	7-6=1

Challenge 94:

Let's assume that all of the students have the name John. So, to answer the questions, all of them have written 20. In this case, the teacher kept none of the answers.

If none of the students have the same name, they all answer 0. And the teacher won't keep any answer.

Let's assume that only one of them has a different name. Then, in this case, 20 students wrote 19 and one wrote 0. The teacher kept the last one.

The maximum number of answers that the teacher kept was one.

Challenge 95: C

To answer this question, we need to find the pattern. From 1 to 10, there is one number 2. From 10 to 19 has the same situation. From 20 to 29, there are 11 number 2. Why? (Consider 22)

With the same method, there is one number 2 in every ten numbers from 30 to 100. So, there are 20 number 2 from 1 to 100. There are 20 number 2 from 100 to 199.

From 200 to 300, there are 120 number 2. Why? (all numbers from 200 to 299 begin with 2)

From 300 to 500 there are 40 number 2. Therefore, there are 200 number 2 from number 1 to 500.

Challenge 96: B

The first possible date of the competition is the soonest when Saturday is the first day of the month. In this case, the third Saturday would be on 15th of May.

Challenge 97: 64

To find the answer, we can factorize numbers from 1, one by one. But, it takes for ever!

Every integer N is the product of powers of prime numbers:

$N = P^a Q^b ... R^y$

Where P, Q, ...,R are prime numbers and a, b, ..., y are positive integers.

If N is a power of a prime, then $N = p^{\alpha}$, therefore, it has $\alpha + 1$ factors.

If $N = P^a Q^b ... R^y$, then, N has $(a+1)(b+1) ... (y+1)$ factors.

To find the smallest number that has 7 factors, first write the factors of seven: $7 = 1 \times 7$

It means that the number in this question has just one prime factor in its decomposition - one with the exponent of $\alpha = 6$. Keep in mind that $b = 0$, and $Q^b = Q^0 = 1$

$N = P^6 Q^0$. To make N as small as possible, we have to choose the smallest available prime 2. The answer is obviously $N = 2^6 = 64$.

The seven factors of 64 are: 1, 2, 4, 8, 16, 32 and 64

Challenge 98: C

The formula for N people to sit in a straight line is N! and at a round table there is (n-1)!.

There are six people. So, the number of different ways to sit them is 6! = 720

From these 720 ways, we must subtract the number of ways that Ann and Bea can sit next to each other.

The cases we need to subtract from whole are the ways of seating 5 persons and one "pair". That would be 5! or 5 × 4 × 3 × 2 × 1 = 120

However, there are two ways Ann and Bea could sit, Ann left of Bea or Bea left of Ann.

So, we double 120 ways to 240 ways.

Answer: 720 – 240 = 480

Challenge 99: 9360

For a positive integer to be divisible by those numbers, it must be divisible by their Least common multiple:

Factorize the numbers to find their Least Common Multiple.

$16 = 2^4$

$36 = 2^2 \times 3^2$

$45 = 3^2 \times 5$

$80 = 2^4 \times 5$

Least Common Multiple = $2^4 \times 3^2 \times 5 = 720$

Every multiple of 720 is divisible by all those above.

Every multiple of 720 can be written as 720n, where n is an integer. The largest 4-digit integer is 9999. Therefore:

720n ≤ 9999 → n ≤ $\frac{9999}{720}$ → n ≤ 13.8875 → n = 13 →

720n = 9360

Challenge 100:

First, notice rule 3 (The product of the four digits is divisible by 10) tells you that one digit must be 5 and none of them should be 0.

Since we're looking for the greatest four digit integer we need to start with 9, which is the greatest digit. If the first digit is 9, then all the three other digits should add up to 9.

One digit is 5 and there is no 0. Therefore, there are two possible ways:

5 + 3 + 1 = 9

5 + 2 + 2 = 9

None of these solutions work. Because, in the first one, there is no even number and it's not divisible by 10. In the second one, digit 2 repeated.

Therefore, 9 is not the first digit. Let's try 8.

If 8 is the first digit. Then:

5 + 2 + 1 = 8

5 + 3 + 0 = 8

The second one has 0, so the only solution is the first one. The number has digits 8, 5, 2, and 1. The greatest such number is 8521

Critical Thinking 1: 204

This question implies "squares of any size". You can find squares of 1 by 1, 2 by 2, 3 by 3 and so on. A chessboard is a square of 8 by 8 and hence there are 64 (8 x 8 = 64) 1 by 1 square on a chessboard.

The next size square is a 2 by 2 unit square. First, find all 2 by 2 squares in the first two rows. You can find seven of them. Then, consider rows 2 and 3. Again, you can find seven. Consider rows 3-4, 4-5, 5-6, 6-7, and 7-8. You'll find seven 2 by 2 squares for each pair. Therefore, there are 7 × 7 = 49 squares of 2 by 2.

We can use the same pattern for the squares of 3×3. You can find six squares of 3×3 in the first 3 rows. Then, consider rows of 2-3-4, 3-4-5, and so on. You'll find 6 × 6 = 36 squares of 3 by 3.

Continue the pattern for other size of square.

64 squares of 1 × 1

49 squares of 2 × 2

36 squares of 3 × 3

25 squares of 4 × 4

16 squares of 5 × 5

9 squares of 6 × 6

4 squares of 7 × 7

1 square of 8 × 8

Total number of squares:

64 + 49 + 36 + 25 + 16 + 9 + 4 + 1 = 204

Critical Thinking 2: 5

For this question, don't try to use the pattern! The first equation says that 1 equals to 5^1, which equals to 5.

1 equals to 5. Therefore, 5 also equals to 1.

$1 = 5^1$
$2 = 5^2$
$3 = 5^3$
$4 = 5^4$
$5 = 1$

Critical Thinking 3:

First, let's find some values of y. Let's choose the smallest possible value for the quotient. It's 0. Then, the remainder should also be 0. Therefore, the number y should be 0.

0 × 7 + 0 = 0

To find the next value of y, you should choose 1 for both quotient and remainder. Then, the value of y is 8.

1 × 7 + 1 = 8

What is the next value of y?

It's 16. 2 × 7 + 2 = 16

Using the same pattern, you can find other values of y.

3 × 7 + 3 = 24

4 × 7 + 4 = 32

5 × 7 + 5 = 40

6 × 7 + 6 = 48

It is possible to choose 7 for both quotient and remainder?

Since, the remainder cannot be equal to the divisor (it's 7 here), therefore, the greatest number you can choose for both quotient and remainder is 6. Then, the greatest value of y is 48.

When you divide 48 by 7, both quotient and remainder are 6.

Critical Thinking 4: 11

To answer this question, we need to find the pattern. For these equations, don't try to find a relationship between numbers on both sides. Instead, consider the digits of each number and try to find a relationship between the two digits of the number in the left side. What operation between the digits of the number in the left side can create the digits of the number of the ride side?

12 = 13   35 = 28   47 = 311   10 = ?

Find the difference of two digits of the number in the left side. That is the left digit of the number in the right side.

The digit (or digits) in the right side of the answer is created by adding the two digits of the first number. For example, 12 = 13

Difference of 2 and 1 is 1 and the sum of 1 and 2 is 3.

Therefore, the answer is 11.

1 − 0 = 1 and 1 + 0 = 1

Critical Thinking 5: 54

One way to answer to this question is considering all three digits numbers and find those that follow the rules. Another way is finding the pattern.

The hundreds digit equals to other digits. Let's start with 1 as hundreds digit. 1 equals to sum of 1 and 0. We can find two such numbers; 101 and 110.

Now, let's consider 2. Number 2 equals to the sum of 1 and 1 or 2 and 0. We can find one number for the first and two numbers for the second pair. 211, 202 and 220.

Number 3 equals to the sum of 3 and 0 or 2 and 1. Therefore, the numbers are 303, 330, 312, 321

Number 4 equals to the sum of 4 and 0, or 3 and 1, or 2 and 2.

The numbers are: 404, 440, 413, 431, 422.

With the same method, we can find the following numbers for 5 as hundreds digit:

505, 550, 514, 541, 532, 523.

For number 6 as hundred digits:

606, 660, 615, 651, 624, 642, 633

Now, use the pattern:

For 1 as hundreds place, there are 2 numbers.

For 2 as hundreds place, there are 3 numbers.

For 3 as hundreds place, there are 4 numbers.

For 4 as hundreds place, there are 5 numbers.

....

Therefore, the total three digits numbers in which the hundreds digit is equal to the sum of other digits equals to:

2 + 3 + 4 + 5 + 6 + 7 + 8 + 9 + 10 = 54

Critical Thinking 6: $X = \frac{27}{70} y$

For this question, try to write an equation. Remember, you need to change percent to decimal. Then, solve for x.

20% of 35% of $\frac{2}{3}$ of variable x equals to 15% of 12% of $\frac{3}{2}$ y.

$0.20 \times 0.35 \times \frac{2}{3} X = 0.15 \times 0.12 \times \frac{3}{2} y$

$$X = \frac{0.15 \times 0.12 \times \frac{3}{2} y}{0.20 \times 0.35 \times \frac{2}{3}} \Rightarrow X = \frac{0.018 \times \frac{3}{2} y}{0.07 \times \frac{2}{3}} \Rightarrow X = \frac{27}{70} y$$

Critical Thinking 7: $\frac{1}{100}$

First, simplify the expression.

$$(1 - \frac{1}{2}) \times (1 - \frac{1}{3}) \times (1 - \frac{1}{4}) \times \ldots \times (1 - \frac{1}{100}) = ?$$

$$(\frac{1}{2}) \times (\frac{2}{3}) \times (\frac{3}{4}) \times \ldots \times (\frac{99}{100}) = \frac{1 \times 2 \times 3 \times \ldots \times 99}{2 \times 3 \times 4 \times \ldots \times 100}$$

Remove the same numbers from both numerator and denominator. For example, cancel out 2, 3, 4, ... from both numerator and denominator. You'll get: $\frac{1}{100}$

Critical Thinking 8: -2

Solve for x:

$$5^x + 5^{x+1} + 5^{x+2} = \frac{31}{25}$$

The common factor is 5^x. Then,

$$5^x (1 + 5^1 + 5^2) = \frac{31}{25} \Rightarrow 5^x (31) = \frac{31}{25} \Rightarrow 5^x = \frac{\frac{31}{25}}{31} \Rightarrow$$

$$5^x = \frac{31}{25} \div \frac{31}{1} = \frac{31}{25} \times \frac{1}{31} = \frac{1}{25}$$

$\frac{1}{25} = 5^{-2}$ Then: $5^x = 5^{-2} \Rightarrow x = -2$

Critical Thinking 9: 9

The average of five numbers is 11. Therefore, their sum is:

5 × 11 = 55

The average of eight numbers is 7.75. Therefore, their sum is:

8 × 7.75 = 62

The sum of all 13 numbers is 55 + 62 = 117

Therefore, the average of these 13 numbers is:

117 ÷ 13 = 9

Critical Thinking 10: 25%

Amanda can paint the room by herself in 8 hours. Therefore, she can paint $\frac{1}{8}$ of the room in an hour. In the same way, Dani can paint $\frac{1}{x}$ of the room in an hour. Together, they can paint $\frac{1}{6}$ part of the room in an hour. Now, write the equation and solve for x.

$$\frac{1}{8} + \frac{1}{x} = \frac{1}{6} \Rightarrow \frac{1}{x} = \frac{1}{6} - \frac{1}{8} = \frac{1}{24} \Rightarrow x = 24$$

Dani can paint the room in 24 hours. Then, in six hours, Dani paints $\frac{6}{24}$ or $\frac{1}{4}$ part or 25% of the room.

Critical Thinking 11: 15 degrees

The clock is a circle and the hour hand moves around it every 12 hours. The clock is 360 degrees divided into 12 hours. So, it's 30 degrees per hour. The hour hand points exactly at the 6 at 6:00, so 30 minutes later, when the minute hand points at the 6, the hour hand is pointing at 6.5 or 15 degrees past 6.

Critical Thinking 12: 343

Find the pattern. First, try to find the relationship between the first and second numbers, 3 and 7.

7 is 3 plus 4, it's also twice of 3 plus 1, or it's three times of 3 minus 2, or 4 times of 3 minus 5.

Now, check the relationships with other numbers. For example 7 and 23.

23 is 7 plus 16. It's also twice of 7 plus 9, or three times of seven plus 2, or four times of 7 minus 5. The last relationship is common for both 3 – 7 and 7 – 21.

Four times of 23 minus 5 is 87. Bingo!!

Therefore, the answer is: $4 \times 87 - 5 = 343$

Critical Thinking 13: 120

Similar to critical thinking number 4, don't try to find a relationship between numbers on both sides. Instead, consider the digits of each number and try to find a relationship between the two digits of the number in the left side. Try to find an operation between the digits of the number in the left side that can create the digits of the number of the ride side.

3 * 4 = 12

2 * 5 = 30

4 * 7 = 84

5 * 8 = ??

For the first equation, the product or 3 and 4 is 12, which is the answer.

For the second equation, the product of 2 and 5 is 10. But, the answer is 30. So, the symbol * is not a multiplication. 10 times 3 is 30.

Let's find the pattern. We know that 3 * 4 = 12 and

2 * 5 = 30.

12 times what number is 12? It's 1. So, $3 \times 4 \times 1 = 12$ and $2 \times 5 \times 3 = 30$

In the first equation, we should find number 1 from 3 and 4. In the second equation, we need to find 3 from 2 and 5. In fact, the difference of 3 and 4 is 1 and the difference of 2 and 5 is 3!

For the third equation, the product of 4 and 7 is 28. The difference of 4 and 7 is 3. Then:

$4 \times 7 \times 3 = 84$

[155]

Since the difference of 5 and 8 is 3, therefore, the answer to the last equation is:

5 * 8 = 5 × 8 × 3 = 120

Critical Thinking 14: 1 percent

First, change the word problem into a mathematic equation.

What percent of 12 is 12 percent of 1?

Put variable x for "what percent". Then,

$x \times 12 = 12\% \times 1 \Rightarrow 12x = 0.12 \Rightarrow x = \frac{0.12}{12} = 0.01 = 1\%$

Critical Thinking 15: 25

First, find the factor of 1080p. The prime factors of 1080p are:

$2^3 \times 3^3 \times 5 \times p$

In order for $2^3 \times 3^3 \times 5 \times p$ to be a perfect cube, each prime factor must come in sets of triples. Since, we have $2^3 \times 3^3 \times 5$, thus, we only need to change 5 to 5^3. Therefore, p equals to 5^2 or 25.

Critical Thinking 16: C, D, and E

We can find the maximum area of the triangle only when the given sides are placed at right angles. Why?

Let's put 10 as the base and 5 as the height. Then, the area of the triangle is: $\frac{10 \times 5}{2} = 25$

The angle less or more than 90 degrees between the sides reduce the area. (Draw it out for yourself). Hence, the area can be anything between 0 and 25.

Critical Thinking 17: 24

A cube has 12 edges. The formula for the volume and surface area of a cube are:

$V = S^3$ $\qquad$ $SA = 6S^2$

The volume of a cube is one-third of the total surface area of the cube. Thus:

$S^3 = \frac{1}{3} 6S^2$

Remove S^2 from both sides and solve for S.

$S = \frac{1}{3} 6 = 2$

One side of the cube is 2. The sum of all edges is

$2 \times 12 = 24$

Critical Thinking 17: C

The sum of some consecutive integers is 17. Since, 17 is a prime number, then, we cannot find any positive consecutive integers whose sum is 17. Why?

Therefore, we need to consider negative numbers. We know that the sum of two consecutive positive numbers can be 17. Those numbers are 8 and 9.

We are looking for consecutive integers. The sum of negative and positive of a number is zero. For example, the sum of 1 and -1 is 0, or the sum of 2 and -2 is 0.

We found 8 and 9. The other numbers are:

9, 8, 7, 6, 5, 4, 3, 2, 1, 0, -1, -2, -3, -4, -5, -6, -7

The sum of above numbers is 17. Thus, the least number of the integers is 17.

Critical Thinking 19: 15

If p and q are prime numbers, then for $p^m q^n$, the number of divisors is $(m+1)(n+1)$.

Thus the number of divisors for $N^2 \times P^4$ is $(2+1)(4+1) = 15$

Another way to solve this problem is by providing numbers for N and P. Let's put 2 for N and 3 for P. Then, the value of $N^2 \times P^4$ is $2^2 \times 3^4 = 324$

Now, find the factors of 324.

324: 1, 2, 3, 4, 6, 9, 12, 18, 27, 36, 54, 81, 108, 162, 324

324 have 15 factors.

Critical Thinking 20:

First, let's find all three digits that add up to 7.

700, 610, 511, 520, 430, 421, 322, 133

For 7, 0 and 0, we can write only one three digit number which is 700.

For 6, 1 and 0, we can find 106, 160, 601, 610,

For 5, 1, and 1: 115, 151, 511

For 5, 2, and 0: 205, 250, 502, 520

For 4, 3, and 0: 304, 340, 403, 430

For 4, 2, and 1: 124, 142, 214, 241, 412, 421

For 3, 2, and 2: 223, 232, 322

For 1, 3, and 3: 133, 313, 331

There are 28 three digits numbers that the sum of their digits is 7.

CPSIA information can be obtained
at www.ICGtesting.com
Printed in the USA
LVOW13s0614200917
549387LV00015B/403/P

9 781548 465056